Delicious

pizza

Delicious

pizza

Love Food ® is an imprint of Parragon Books Ltd

Parragon
Queen Street House
4 Queen Street
Bath BA1 1HE, UK

Photography by Günter Beer
Home economy by Stevan Paul
Introduction and new recipes by Linda Doeser

ISBN 978-1-4075-1627-1

Printed in China

Notes for the reader

• This book uses metric and imperial measurements. Follow the same units of measurements throughout; do not mix imperial and metric.
• All spoon measurements are level: teaspoons are assumed to be 5 ml and tablespoons are assumed to be 15 ml.
• Unless otherwise stated, milk is assumed to be low fat and eggs are medium. The times given are an approximate guide only.
• Some recipes contain nuts. If you are allergic to nuts you should avoid using them and any products containing nuts.
• Recipes using raw or very lightly cooked eggs should be avoided by infants, the elderly, pregnant women, convalescents and anyone suffering from illness.

Contents

Introduction

The word pizza comes from the Italian word 'pizzicare,' meaning to be hot or spicy and it is thought that the original pizza consisted of a bread dough base drizzled liberally with olive oil and sprinkled with garlic, oregano and fiery hot peperoncino chillies. It was only in the nineteenth century, when the city of Naples created a pizza to honour Queen Margherita, that tomatoes and cheese – those staples of pizza toppings – were introduced. As Italians, particularly Neapolitans, moved across Europe and North America they opened pizzerias in all the major cities and this humble snack food became a global phenomenon.

Pizza toppings have become increasingly varied and interesting as cooks around the world have experimented with local ingredients. Modern toppings also tend to include more ingredients than the pizzas of the past. If Italy had a queen to honour now,

tomatoes, cheese and basil would probably seem a somewhat inadequate way to commemorate a royal visit. Nevertheless, the classic recipes are still firm favourites with many, as they are quick and easy to prepare and the traditional flavour combinations have stood the test of time.

Making pizza

This book provides a recipe for basic Pizza Dough (see page 11) which takes little time, but it needs to stand for about 1 hour to rise. If you are in a hurry, you can use a ready-made, part-cooked pizza base. These are available from supermarkets and, while not quite as delicious as a homemade one, are still very satisfactory.

Many pizza recipes start by covering the pizza base with some kind of tomato sauce. One of the easiest and most convenient options is to buy a good brand of

ready-made pizza sauce. However, making your own is almost as easy. For a basic Tomato Sauce, soften a chopped onion and a finely chopped garlic clove in a tablespoon of olive oil in a saucepan for 5 minutes. Stir in 200 g/7 oz canned chopped tomatoes, 1–2 teaspoons tomato purée, a pinch of sugar and a pinch of dried oregano, season with salt and pepper and simmer gently, stirring occasionally, for 20–25 minutes, until thick and pulpy. Leave to cool completely before using.

Homemade tomato sauce can be stored in a screw-top jar in the refrigerator for up to a week. You could also use passata and even tomato purée, although this has a very intense flavour and is probably better diluted with a little water first. Peeled and finely diced fresh tomatoes may also be used, creating a different texture. Of course, not all pizzas include tomatoes or tomato sauce.

The recipes in this book suggest a huge variety of different toppings to suit all tastes. They are all easy to follow and have been divided into four chapters, making it easy to find exactly the one you want. Classic Toppings speaks for itself and includes traditional meat, vegetarian and shellfish pizzas. The toppings in Meat Lovers range from creamy chicken to spicy pepperoni and meatballs – the perfect choice when you're really hungry. Strictly Vegetarian suggests some delicious new ways with vegetables as well as some favourite combinations, while the recipes in Something Special are ideal for those days when you want something a little different.

Classic Toppings

serves 2–4

15 g/¹/₂ oz fresh yeast or
1 tsp dried or active dry yeast

6 tbsp lukewarm water

¹/₂ tsp sugar

1 tbsp olive oil, plus extra
for oiling

175 g/6 oz plain flour, plus
extra for dusting

1 tsp salt

pizza dough

Combine the fresh yeast with the water and sugar in a bowl.
If using dried yeast, sprinkle it over the surface of the water
(without the sugar) and whisk in until dissolved.

Set aside in a warm place for 10–15 minutes until frothy on the
surface. Stir in the olive oil.

Sift the flour and salt into a large bowl. If using easy-blend yeast,
stir it in. Make a well in the centre and pour in the yeast liquid.

Using either floured hands or a wooden spoon, mix together to
form a dough. Turn out on to a floured work surface and knead
for about 5 minutes or until smooth and elastic.

Place the dough in a large oiled plastic bag and set aside in a
warm place for about 1 hour or until doubled in size. Airing
cupboards are often the best places for this process, as the
temperature remains constant.

Turn out on to a lightly floured surface and 'knock back' by
punching the dough. This releases any air bubbles which would
make the pizza uneven. Knead 4 or 5 times. The dough is now
ready to use.

serves 2–4

2 tbsp olive oil, plus extra
for brushing

1 quantity Pizza Dough
(see page 11), or 1 x 25-cm/
10-inch pizza base

plain flour, for dusting

6 tomatoes, thinly sliced

175 g/6 oz mozzarella cheese,
drained and thinly sliced

2 tbsp shredded fresh basil
leaves

salt and pepper

Margherita pizza

Preheat the oven to 230°C/450°F/Gas Mark 8. Brush a baking
sheet with oil.

Roll out the dough on a lightly floured surface to a 25-cm/
10-inch round. Place on the baking sheet and push up the edge
a little. Cover and let stand in a warm place for 10 minutes.

Arrange the tomato and mozzarella slices alternately over the
pizza base. Season to taste with salt and pepper, sprinkle with
the basil, and drizzle with the olive oil.

Bake in the oven for 15–20 minutes, until the crust is crisp and
the cheese has melted.

serves 2–4

2 tbsp olive oil, plus extra for brushing

1 quantity Pizza Dough (see page 11), or 1 x 25-cm/ 10-inch pizza base

plain flour, for dusting

400 g/14 oz canned chopped tomatoes

140 g/5 oz ham, diced

200 g/7 oz canned pineapple slices in juice, drained

55 g/2 oz Cheddar cheese, grated

Hawaiian pizza

Preheat the oven to 200°C/400°F/Gas Mark 6. Brush a baking sheet with oil.

Roll out the dough on a lightly floured surface to a 25-cm/ 10-inch round. Place on the baking sheet and push up the edge a little. Cover and let stand in a warm place for 10 minutes.

Spoon the tomatoes over the base almost to the edge, then sprinkle evenly with the ham.

Cut the pineapple slices into bite-sized pieces and sprinkle them over the pizza. Sprinkle with the grated cheese and bake for 20 minutes, until the edge is crisp and golden. Serve immediately.

serves 2–4

olive oil, for brushing

1 quantity Pizza Dough
(see page 11), or 1 x 25-cm/
10-inch pizza base

plain flour, for dusting

2 tbsp butter or margarine

350 g/12 oz mixed
mushrooms, sliced

2 garlic cloves, crushed

2 tbsp chopped fresh parsley,
plus extra to garnish

2 tbsp tomato purée

6 tbsp passata

85 g/3 oz mozzarella cheese,
grated

salt and pepper

garlic mushroom pizza

Preheat the oven to 190°C/375°F/Gas Mark 5. Brush a baking sheet with oil.

Roll out the dough on a lightly floured surface to a 25-cm/ 10-inch round. Place on the baking sheet and push up the edge a little. Cover and let stand in a warm place for 10 minutes.

Melt the butter in a frying pan and cook the mushrooms, garlic and parsley together over a low heat for 5 minutes.

Combine the tomato purée and passata and spoon onto the pizza base, leaving a 1-cm/½-inch edge of dough. Spoon the mushroom mixture on top. Season to taste with salt and pepper and sprinkle the cheese on top.

Cook the pizza in the oven for 20–25 minutes or until the base is crisp and the cheese has melted. Garnish with chopped parsley and serve immediately.

serves 4

2 loaves of ciabatta or
2 baguettes

1 quantity basic Tomato
Sauce (see page 7)

4 plum tomatoes, sliced
thinly lengthways

150 g/5½ oz mozzarella
cheese, thinly sliced

10 black olives, cut into rings

8 fresh basil leaves, shredded

olive oil, for drizzling

salt and pepper

tomato & olive pizzas

Cut the bread in half lengthways and toast the cut side of the bread lightly. Carefully spread the toasted bread with the Tomato Sauce.

Arrange the tomato and mozzarella slices alternately along the length of each toasted slice.

Top with the olive rings and half of the basil. Drizzle over a little olive oil and season with salt and pepper.

Either place under a preheated medium grill and cook until the cheese is melted and bubbling, or bake in an oven preheated to 200°C/400°F/Gas Mark 6 for 15–20 minutes.

Sprinkle over the remaining basil and serve immediately.

serves 2–4

4 tbsp olive oil, plus extra for brushing

140 g/5 oz mushrooms, chopped

1 garlic clove, thinly sliced (optional)

1 tbsp lemon juice

1 quantity Pizza Dough (see page 11), or 1 x 25-cm/ 10-inch pizza base

plain flour, for dusting

140 g/5 oz bacon, diced

pinch of dried oregano

55 g/2 oz Cheddar cheese, grated

salt and pepper

tasty bacon pizza

Heat half the olive oil in a saucepan. Add the mushrooms, garlic and lemon juice, season with salt and pepper, cover and cook over a low heat, stirring occasionally, for 6 minutes. Remove the pan from the heat and leave to cool.

Preheat the oven to 200°C/400°F/Gas Mark 6. Brush a baking sheet with oil.

Roll out the dough on a lightly floured surface to a 25-cm/ 10-inch round. Place on the baking sheet and push up the edge a little. Cover and leave to stand in a warm place for 10 minutes.

Brush the pizza base with half the remaining olive oil and spread out the mushrooms evenly on top almost to the edge. Sprinkle with the diced bacon and season with a pinch of dried oregano. Sprinkle the cheese over the pizza, drizzle with the remaining oil and bake for 20–25 minutes, until crisp and golden. Serve immediately.

serves 2–4

2 tbsp olive oil, plus extra for brushing

1 quantity Pizza Dough (see page 11), or 1 x 25-cm/ 10-inch pizza base

plain flour, for dusting

175 ml/6 fl oz passata or 1 quantity basic Tomato Sauce (see page 7)

1 red onion, halved and thinly sliced

55 g/2 oz Parmesan cheese, freshly grated

55 g/2 oz Gorgonzola cheese

55 g/2 oz fontina cheese, thinly sliced

55 g/2 oz goat's cheese

1 tbsp pine kernels or capers

fresh basil sprigs, to garnish

salt and pepper

quattro fromaggi pizza

Preheat the oven to 200°C/400°F/Gas Mark 6. Brush a baking sheet with oil.

Roll out the dough on a lightly floured surface to a 25-cm/ 10-inch round. Place on the baking sheet and push up the edge a little. Cover and leave to stand in a warm place for 10 minutes.

Brush the pizza base with half the olive oil, then spread the passata or Tomato Sauce over it almost to the edge. Spread out the onion slices evenly over the top and season with salt and pepper.

Cover one-quarter of the pizza base with grated Parmesan. Crumble the Gorgonzola over a second quarter and arrange the slices of fontina over a third quarter. Depending on the type of goat's cheese, either crumble it directly over the remaining quarter or slice it first before adding to the pizza.

Sprinkle the pine kernels over the top and drizzle with the remaining olive oil. Bake for 20–25 minutes, until crisp and golden. Garnish with basil sprigs and serve immediately.

serves 2–4

6–8 canned anchovy fillets, drained and halved lengthways

2 tbsp milk (optional)

4 tbsp olive oil, plus extra for brushing

1 onion, halved and thinly sliced

2 garlic cloves, finely chopped

400 g/14 oz canned chopped tomatoes

1 tbsp sun-dried tomato paste

pinch of dried oregano

1 tbsp chopped fresh flat-leaf parsley

1 quantity Pizza Dough (see page 11), or 1 x 25-cm/ 10-inch pizza base

plain flour, for dusting

175 g/6 oz mozzarella cheese, thinly sliced

4–6 pimiento stuffed olives, sliced

salt and pepper

anchovy pizza

If you find anchovies too salty, put them in a shallow saucer, add the milk and leave to soak for 10 minutes. Drain and pat dry with kitchen paper.

Meanwhile, heat 2 tablespoons of the olive oil in a saucepan. Add the onion and cook over a low heat, stirring occasionally, for 5 minutes, until softened. Stir in the garlic and cook for a further 2 minutes, then add the tomatoes, sun-dried tomato paste and oregano and season with salt and pepper. Simmer gently, stirring occasionally, for 15–20 minutes, until thickened. Remove the pan from the heat, stir in the parsley and leave to cool.

Preheat the oven to 200°C/400°F/Gas Mark 6. Brush a baking sheet with oil.

Roll out the dough on a lightly floured surface to a 25-cm/ 10-inch round. Place on the baking sheet and push up the edge a little. Cover and leave to stand in a warm place for 10 minutes.

Brush the pizza base with half the remaining oil, then cover evenly with the cooled tomato sauce, spreading it out almost to the edge. Place the slices of mozzarella on top. Make a lattice pattern with the halved anchovy fillets and place a slice of olive on the spaces between. Drizzle with the remaining oil and bake for 20–25 minutes, until crisp and golden. Serve immediately.

serves 2–4

3 tbsp olive oil, plus extra for
brushing and drizzling

1 quantity Pizza Dough
(see page 11), or 1 x 25-cm/
10-inch pizza base

plain flour, for dusting

1 quantity basic Tomato
Sauce (see page 7)

2 tbsp freshly grated
Parmesan cheese

175 g/6 oz fresh spinach

1 small red onion, thinly
sliced

1/4 tsp freshly grated nutmeg

2 hard-boiled eggs

15 g/1/2 oz fresh white
breadcrumbs

55 g/2 oz Jarlsberg, Cheddar
or Gruyère cheese, grated

2 tbsp flaked almonds

salt and pepper

Florentine pizza

Preheat the oven to 200°C/400°F/Gas Mark 6. Brush a baking
sheet with oil.

Roll out the dough on a lightly floured surface to a 25-cm/
10-inch round. Place on the baking sheet and push up the
edge a little. Cover and let stand in a warm place for 10 minutes.
Spread the Tomato Sauce almost to the edge and sprinkle the
Parmesan over it.

Remove the stalks from the spinach and wash the leaves
thoroughly in plenty of cold water. Drain well and pat off the
excess water with kitchen paper.

Heat the remaining oil and cook the onion for 5 minutes until
softened. Add the spinach and cook until just wilted. Drain off
any excess liquid. Arrange on the pizza and sprinkle over the
nutmeg and sprinkle the Parmesan over it.

Shell and slice the eggs. Arrange the slices of egg on top of the
spinach.

Combine the breadcrumbs, cheese and almonds, and sprinkle
over. Drizzle with a little olive oil and season to taste.

Bake for 18–20 minutes, or until the edge is crisp and golden.
Serve the pizza immediately.

serves 2–4

2 tbsp olive oil, plus extra for brushing

1 quantity Pizza Dough (see page 11), or 1 x 25-cm/ 10-inch pizza base

plain flour, for dusting

400 g/14 oz canned chopped tomatoes

200 g/7 oz canned tuna in olive oil, drained

140 g/5 oz cooked peeled prawns

100 g/3½ oz mozzarella cheese, grated

1 tbsp chopped fresh parsley

1 tbsp chopped fresh oregano

1 garlic clove, very finely chopped

seafood pizza

Preheat the oven to 200°C/400°F/Gas Mark 6. Brush a baking sheet with oil.

Roll out the dough on a lightly floured surface to a 25-cm/ 10-inch round. Place on the baking sheet and push up the edge a little. Cover and let stand in a warm place for 10 minutes.

Spoon the tomatoes evenly over the base almost to the edge. Flake the tuna and spread it over the tomatoes, then arrange the prawns on top. Sprinkle with the mozzarella.

Mix together the parsley, oregano, garlic and olive oil, and drizzle the mixture over the pizza. Bake for 20 minutes, until the edge is crisp and golden. Serve immediately.

Meat Lovers

serves 2–4

olive oil, for brushing and drizzling

1 quantity Pizza Dough (see page 11), or 1 x 25-cm/10-inch pizza base

plain flour, for dusting

4 tbsp sun-dried tomato paste

4 tomatoes, skinned and thinly sliced

salt

2 red onions, chopped finely

4 slices prosciutto or other cooked ham, coarsely shredded

12 slices pepperoni sausage

12 black olives

3/4 tsp dried oregano

55 g/2 oz mozzarella cheese, grated

pepperoni & onion pizza

Preheat the oven to 220°C/425°F/Gas Mark 7. Brush a baking sheet with oil.

Roll out the dough on a lightly floured surface to a 25-cm/10-inch round. Place on the baking sheet and push up the edge a little. Cover and let stand in a warm place for 10 minutes.

Spread the sun-dried tomato paste evenly over the base. Arrange the tomato slices on the base and season with salt. Sprinkle over the chopped onion and prosciutto and arrange the pepperoni on top. Add the olives and sprinkle with oregano. Then add the grated cheese, and drizzle with olive oil.

Bake in the oven for 20–30 minutes, until golden and sizzling. Serve immediately.

serves 2–4

4 tbsp olive oil, plus extra for
brushing

1 quantity Pizza Dough
(see page 11), or 1 x 25-cm/
10-inch pizza base

plain flour, for dusting

2 shallots, thinly sliced

1 yellow pepper, deseeded
and cut into thin strips

115 g/4 oz chestnut
mushrooms, thinly sliced

350 g/12 oz skinless, boneless
chicken breasts portions, cut
into thin strips

2 tbsp chopped fresh parsley

175 g/6 oz mozzarella cheese,
grated

salt and pepper

chicken & mushroom pizza

Preheat the oven to 200°C/400°F/Gas Mark 6. Brush a baking
sheet with oil.

Roll out the dough on a lightly floured surface to a 25-cm/
10-inch round. Place on the baking sheet and push up the edge
a little. Cover and let stand in a warm place for 10 minutes.

Heat 2 tablespoon of olive oil in a wok or large frying pan. Add
the shallots, yellow pepper, mushrooms and chicken, and stir-fry
over a medium-high heat for 4–5 minutes. Remove the mixture
with a slotted spoon and leave to cool.

Brush the pizza with 1 tablespoon of olive oil. Stir the parsley
into the chicken and mushroom mixture and season with salt
and pepper. Spread the mixture evenly over the pizza base
almost to the edge. Sprinkle with the mozzarella, drizzle over
the remaining olive oil, and bake for 20 minutes, until the edge is
crisp and golden. Serve immediately.

serves 2–4

2 tbsp olive oil, plus extra for
brushing

1 quantity Pizza Dough
(see page 11), or 1 x 25-cm/
10-inch pizza base

plain flour, for dusting

200 g/7 oz chorizo or other
spicy sausages

55 g/2 oz freshly grated
Parmesan cheese

400 g/14 oz canned chopped
tomatoes

115 g/4 oz pancetta or bacon,
cut into thin slices

1 tbsp fresh basil leaves

sausage pizza

Preheat the oven to 200°C/400°F/Gas Mark 6. Brush a baking
sheet with oil.

Roll out the dough on a lightly floured surface to a 25-cm/
10-inch round. Place on the baking sheet and push up the edge
a little. Cover and let stand in a warm place for 10 minutes.

Remove and discard the sausage casings and crumble the meat
into a bowl. Add the Parmesan and mix well.

Spoon the tomatoes evenly over the pizza base almost to the
edge, then sprinkle with the sausage mixture. Top with the
pancetta and basil leaves, and drizzle with the olive oil. Bake for
20 minutes, until the edge is crisp and golden. Serve immediately.

serves 2–4

2 tbsp olive oil, plus extra for brushing

1 bunch of spring onions, chopped

2 garlic cloves, finely chopped

225g/8 oz minced beef

1 tsp chilli powder

200 g/7 oz canned chopped tomatoes

1/2 tsp Tabasco sauce

200 g/7 oz canned red kidney beans, drained and rinsed

1 quantity Pizza Dough (see page 11), or 1 x 25-cm/ 10-inch pizza base

plain flour, for dusting

2–3 jalapeño chillies, thinly sliced

150 g/5 oz mozzarella cheese, grated

salt and pepper

chilli pizza

Heat the oil in a saucepan. Add the spring onions and cook over a medium-low heat, stirring occasionally, for 4–5 minutes, until softened. Add the garlic, minced beef and chilli powder and cook, stirring occasionally, for 5 minutes, until browned. Stir in the tomatoes and Tabasco and bring to the boil. Lower the heat, cover and simmer for 30 minutes, then remove the pan from the heat, stir in the beans, season with salt and pepper and leave to cool.

Preheat the oven to 200°C/400°F/Gas Mark 6. Brush a baking sheet with oil.

Roll out the dough on a lightly floured surface to a 10-inch/ 25-cm round. Place on the baking sheet and push up the edge a little. Cover and let stand in a warm place for 10 minutes.

Spoon the meat mixture evenly over the pizza base almost to the edge. Sprinkle with the chillies and mozzarella and bake for 20 minutes, until the edge is crisp and golden. Serve immediately.

serves 2–4

2 tbsp olive oil, plus extra for brushing

1 quantity Pizza Dough (see page 11), or 1 x 25-cm/ 10-inch pizza base

plain flour, for dusting

2 tbsp sun-dried tomato paste

150 g/5 oz mozzarella cheese, torn into small pieces

400 g/14 oz canned chopped tomatoes

70 g/2¹/₂ oz ham, cut into thin strips

2 garlic cloves, finely chopped

¹/₂ red pepper, deseeded and thinly sliced

6 stoned black olives, halved

1 tbsp fresh basil leaves

2 tbsp freshly grated Parmesan cheese

ham & tomato pizza

Preheat the oven to 200°C/400°F/Gas Mark 6. Brush a baking sheet with oil.

Roll out the dough on a lightly floured surface to a 25-cm/ 10-inch round. Place on the baking sheet and push up the edge a little. Cover and let stand in a warm place for 10 minutes.

Spread the sun-dried tomato paste over the base almost to the edge. Sprinkle with half the mozzarella. Spoon the tomatoes evenly over the top, then sprinkle with the ham, garlic, red pepper, olives and basil leaves.

Add the remaining mozzarella, drizzle with the olive oil and sprinkle evenly with the Parmesan. Bake for 20 minutes, until the edge is crisp and golden. Serve immediately.

serves 2–4

2 tbsp olive oil, plus extra for brushing

1 quantity Pizza Dough (see page 11), or 1 x 25-cm/ 10-inch pizza base

plain flour, for dusting

5 tbsp basic Tomato Sauce (see page 7)

150 g/5 oz pepperoni, sliced

4–5 jalapeño chillies in brine, drained and thinly sliced

1 small green pepper, deseeded and cut into thin strips

55 g/2 oz mozzarella cheese, sliced

55 g/2 oz Cheddar cheese, grated

extra-spicy pepperoni pizza

Preheat the oven to 200°C/400°F/Gas Mark 6. Brush a baking sheet with oil.

Roll out the dough on a lightly floured surface to a 25-cm/ 10-inch round. Place on the baking sheet and push up the edge a little. Cover and let stand in a warm place for 10 minutes.

Spread the Tomato Sauce evenly over the base almost to the edge. Arrange the pepperoni slices on top and sprinkle with the chillies and green pepper. Arrange the mozzarella slices over the pepperoni and sprinkle with the Cheddar.

Drizzle with the olive oil and bake for 20 minutes, until the edge is crisp and golden. Serve immediately.

serves 2–4

250 g/9 oz flaky pastry dough, well chilled

plain flour, for dusting

3 tbsp butter

1 red onion, chopped

1 garlic clove, chopped

5 tbsp plain white flour

300 ml/10 fl oz milk

50 g/1³/4 oz finely grated Parmesan cheese, plus extra for sprinkling

2 eggs, hard-boiled, cut into quarters

100 g/3¹/2 oz Italian pork sausage, such as Felino salami, cut into strips

fresh thyme sprigs, to garnish

salt and pepper

mini creamy ham pizzas

Fold the pastry in half and grate it into 4 individual flan tins measuring 10 cm/4 inches across. Using a floured fork, press the pastry flakes down evenly, making sure that there are no holes and that the pastry comes up the sides of the tins.

Line with foil and bake blind in a preheated oven, 220°C/425°F/Gas Mark 7, for 10 minutes. Reduce the heat to 200°C/400°F/Gas Mark 6, remove the foil and cook for a further 15 minutes, or until golden and set.

Heat the butter in a saucepan. Add the onion and garlic and cook for 5–6 minutes, or until softened.

Add the flour, stirring well to coat the onion and garlic. Gradually stir in the milk to make a thick sauce.

Season the sauce with salt and pepper to taste, then stir in the Parmesan. Do not reheat once the cheese has been added or the sauce will become too stringy.

Spread the sauce over the cooked pastry cases. Decorate with the eggs and strips of sausage.

Sprinkle with a little extra Parmesan, return to the oven and bake for 5 minutes, just to heat through.

Serve immediately, garnished with sprigs of fresh thyme.

serves 2–4

2 tbsp olive oil, plus extra for brushing

2–4 fresh or pickled jalapeño chillies, thinly sliced

1 quantity Pizza Dough (see page 11), or 1 x 25-cm/ 10-inch pizza base

plain flour, for dusting

125–175 ml/4–6 fl oz smoky barbecue sauce

4 tomatoes, sliced

salt

85 g/3 oz smoked ham, diced

85 g/3 oz pepperoni, thinly sliced

55 g/2 oz Gruyère cheese, grated

Chicago pepperoni pizza

Preheat the oven to 200°C/400°F/Gas 6. Brush a baking sheet with oil. Deseed the chillies if you prefer a milder flavour.

Roll out the dough on a lightly floured surface to a 25-cm/ 10-inch round. Place on the baking sheet and push up the edge a little. Cover and leave to stand in a warm place for 10 minutes.

Brush the pizza base with half the oil, then spread the barbecue sauce evenly over it almost to the edge. Arrange the tomato slices over the base and season with salt, then sprinkle with the smoked ham. Cover with the pepperoni slices, top with the chillies and sprinkle with the cheese. Drizzle with the remaining oil and bake for 20–25 minutes, until crisp and golden. Serve immediately.

serves 2–4

4 tbsp olive oil, plus extra for
brushing

55 g/2 oz smoked bacon,
diced

1 onion, finely chopped

280 g/10 oz skinless and
boneless chicken breasts
portions, cut into strips

1 tsp chopped fresh tarragon

115 g/4 oz sliced smoked
chicken, cut into strips

1½ quantity Pizza Dough
(see page 11), or 1 x 38-cm/
15-inch pizza base

plain flour for dusting

pinch of dried oregano

140 g/5 oz mozzarella cheese,
grated

deep-pan chicken feast pizza

Heat 2 tablespoons of the oil with the bacon in a frying pan. Add the onion and cook over a low heat, stirring occasionally, for 5 minutes, until softened. Add the fresh chicken strips, increase the heat to medium and stir-fry for 4–5 minutes, until lightly browned on the outside.

Remove the pan from the heat and drain off as much oil as possible. Stir in the tarragon and leave to cool completely. Then add the smoked chicken strips.

Preheat the oven to 220°C/425°F/Gas Mark 7. Brush a baking sheet or deep pizza pan with oil.

Roll out the dough on a lightly floured surface to a 38-cm/ 15-inch round. Place on the baking sheet, push up the edge and roll it over a little. Cover and leave to stand in a warm place for 10 minutes.

Brush the pizza base with 1 tablespoon of oil, then spoon on the chicken mixture and sprinkle with the oregano. Drizzle with the remaining oil and sprinkle with the mozzarella. Bake for 25–30 minutes, until golden. Serve immediately.

serves 2–4

5 tbsp olive oil, plus extra for brushing

2 onions, thinly sliced

40 g/1½ oz butter

1 tbsp plain flour, plus extra for dusting

125 ml/4 fl oz milk

pinch of grated nutmeg

200 g/7 oz lean minced beef

25 g/1 oz ham, finely chopped

1 tbsp chopped fresh flat-leaf parsley

55 g/2 oz Parmesan cheese, grated

1 egg yolk

1 quantity Pizza Dough (see page 11), or 1 x 25-cm/10-inch pizza base

1 quantity basic Tomato Sauce (see page 7)

8 black olives

115 g/4 oz mozzarella cheese, grated

salt and pepper

meatball pizza

Preheat the oven to 200°C/400°F/Gas Mark 6. Brush a baking sheet with oil. Heat 2 tablespoon of the oil in a frying pan. Add the onions and cook over a low heat, stirring occasionally, for 15–20 minutes, until golden brown.

Meanwhile, make a béchamel sauce; melt 1 tablespoon of the butter in a small saucepan. Stir in the flour and cook, stirring constantly, for 1 minute. Gradually stir in the milk and bring to the boil, stirring constantly. Cook, stirring, for 1–2 minutes more, until thickened. Remove the pan from the heat and stir in a small pinch of nutmeg.

Mix together the minced beef, ham, parsley, Parmesan and egg yolk in a bowl and season. Add 1–2 tablespoon of the béchamel and bring the mixture together. Shape into about 12 small balls and dust lightly with flour. Melt the remaining butter with 1 tablespoon of the remaining oil in another frying pan. Add the meatballs and cook over a medium heat, turning frequently, for 4–5 minutes, until browned all over. Remove with a slotted spoon and set aside.

Roll out the dough on a lightly floured surface to a 25-cm/10-inch round. Place on the baking sheet and push up the edge a little. Cover and leave to stand in a warm place for 10 minutes.

Brush the pizza base with half the remaining olive oil. Spread the Tomato Sauce over the base almost to the edge. Using a slotted spoon, add the onions evenly over the top. Arrange the meatballs on top of the onions and add the olives, then sprinkle with the mozzarella and drizzle with the remaining oil. Bake for 20 minutes, until crisp and golden. Serve immediately.

Strictly Vegetarian

serves 2–4

125 ml/4 fl oz olive oil, plus
extra for brushing

4 garlic cloves

2 red onions, cut into wedges

1 orange pepper, deseeded
and cut into 8 strips

1 yellow pepper, deseeded
and cut into 8 strips

4 baby courgettes, halved
lengthways

4 baby aubergines, cut
lengthways into 4 slices

1 tbsp balsamic vinegar

2 tbsp fresh basil leaves,

1 quantity Pizza Dough
(see page 11), or 1 x 25-cm/
10-inch pizza base

plain flour, for dusting

1 quantity basic Tomato
Sauce (see page 7)

175 g/6 oz goat's cheese,
diced

salt and pepper

roasted vegetable pizza

Preheat the oven to 200°C/400°F/Gas Mark 6. Brush a baking sheet with oil.

Spread the garlic, onions, peppers, courgettes and aubergines in a roasting tin. Season to taste with salt and pepper. Mix the oil, vinegar and basil together in a jug and pour the mixture over the vegetables, tossing well to coat. Roast in the preheated oven for 15 minutes, turning once or twice during cooking. Leave to cool. Increase the oven temperature to 220°C/425°F/Gas Mark 7.

Roll out the dough on a lightly floured surface to a 25-cm/ 10-inch round. Place on the baking sheet and push up the edge a little. Cover and let stand in a warm place for 10 minutes.

Add the Tomato Sauce to the pizza base, spreading it almost to the edges. Peel off the skins from the pepper strips. Peel and slice the garlic. Arrange the vegetables on top of the Tomato Sauce, then sprinkle with the goat's cheese. Drizzle over the roasting juices.

Bake for 15–20 minutes, or until golden. Garnish with fresh basil and serve immediately.

serves 8

1 quantity Pizza Dough
(see page 11) or 1 x 25-cm/
10-inch pizza base

plain flour, for dusting

2 tbsp olive oil, plus extra for
oiling and drizzling

1/2 red pepper, deseeded and
thinly sliced

1/2 green pepper, deseeded
and thinly sliced

1/2 yellow pepper, deseeded
and thinly sliced

1 small red onion, thinly
sliced

1 garlic clove, crushed

1 quantity basic Tomato
Sauce (see page 7)

3 tbsp golden raisins

4 tbsp pine kernels

1 tbsp chopped fresh thyme

salt and pepper

pepper & onion
pizza fingers

Preheat the oven to 200°C/400°F/Gas Mark 6.

Roll out or press the dough, using a rolling pin or your hands,
on a lightly floured work surface to fit a 30 x 18-cm/12 x 7-inch
oiled Swiss roll tin. Place the dough in the tin and push up the
edges slightly.

Cover with clingfilm and set the dough aside in a warm place for
about 10 minutes to rise slightly.

Heat the oil in a large frying pan. Add the peppers, onion and
garlic and cook gently for 5 minutes until they have softened.
Set aside to cool.

Spread the Tomato Sauce over the base of the pizza almost
to the edge. Sprinkle over the golden raisins and top with the
cooled pepper mixture. Add the pine kernels and thyme. Drizzle
with a little olive oil and season to taste with salt and pepper.

Bake for 18–20 minutes, or until the edges are crisp and golden.
Cut into fingers and serve immediately.

serves 2–4

3 tbsp oil, plus extra for brushing

1 quantity Pizza Dough (see page 11), or 1 x 25-cm/10-inch pizza base

plain flour, for dusting

2 garlic cloves, crushed

2 tbsp chopped fresh oregano

85 g/3 oz curd cheese

1 tbsp milk

40 g/1½ oz butter

350 g/12 oz mixed mushrooms, sliced

2 tsp lemon juice

1 tbsp chopped fresh marjoram

4 tbsp freshly grated Parmesan cheese

salt and pepper

mixed mushroom pizza

Preheat the oven to 240°C/475°F/Gas Mark 9. Brush a baking sheet with oil.

Roll out the dough on a lightly floured surface to a 25-cm/10-inch round. Place on the baking sheet and push up the edge a little. Cover and let stand in a warm place for 10 minutes.

Mix 2 tablespoons of the oil, the garlic and oregano together and brush over the pizza base.

Mix the curd cheese and milk together in a bowl. Season to taste with salt and pepper and spread the mixture over the pizza base, leaving a 4-cm/1½-inch border.

Heat the butter and remaining oil together in a large frying pan. Add the mushrooms and cook over a high heat for 2 minutes. Remove the frying pan from the heat, season to taste with salt and pepper and stir in the lemon juice and marjoram.

Spoon the mushroom mixture over the pizza base, leaving a 1-cm/½-inch border. Sprinkle with the grated Parmesan, then bake in the oven for 12–15 minutes, until the crusts are crisp and the mushrooms are cooked. Serve immediately.

serves 2–4

olive oil, for brushing

1 quantity Pizza Dough
(see page 11), or 1 x 25-cm/
10-inch pizza base

plain flour, for dusting

4 tbsp sun-dried tomato
purée

150g/5^1/$_2$ oz ricotta cheese

10 sun-dried tomatoes in oil,
drained

1 tbsp fresh thyme

salt and pepper

tomato & ricotta pizza

Preheat the oven to 200°C/400°F/Gas Mark 6. Brush a baking sheet with oil.

Roll out the dough on a lightly floured surface to a 25-cm/ 10-inch round. Place on the baking sheet and push up the edge a little. Cover and let stand in a warm place for 10 minutes.

Spread the sun-dried tomato purée evenly over the dough, then dot spoonfuls of ricotta cheese on top.

Cut the sun-dried tomatoes into thin strips and arrange these over the top of the pizza.

Finally, sprinkle the fresh thyme leaves over the top of the pizza and season with salt and pepper to taste. Bake for 30 minutes or until the crust is golden. Serve the pizza hot.

serves 4

1 quantity Pizza Dough
(see page 11), or 1 x 25-cm/
10-inch pizza base

olive oil, for brushing

200 g/7 oz canned chopped
tomatoes with garlic and
herbs

2 tbsp tomato purée

200 g/7 oz canned kidney
beans, drained and rinsed

115 g/4 oz sweetcorn kernels,
thawed if frozen

1–2 tsp chilli sauce

1 large red onion, shredded

100 g/3 1/2 oz mature Cheddar
cheese, grated

1 large, fresh green chilli,
deseeded and sliced into
rings

salt and pepper

Mexican pizza

Preheat the oven to 220°C/425°F/Gas Mark 7. Brush a baking
sheet with oil.

Roll out the dough on a lightly floured surface to a 25-cm/
10-inch round. Place on the baking sheet and push up the edge
a little. Cover and let stand in a warm place for 10 minutes.

Mix the chopped tomatoes, tomato purée, kidney beans and
sweetcorn together in a bowl and add chilli sauce to taste.
Season with salt and pepper.

Spread the tomato and kidney bean mixture evenly over the
pizza base. Top the pizza with shredded onion and sprinkle with
some grated Cheddar cheese and a few slices of green chilli, to
taste.

Bake for about 20 minutes, until the vegetables are tender, the
cheese has melted and the base is crisp and golden.

Remove the pizza from the baking tray and transfer to serving
plates. Serve hot.

serves 2–4

olive oil, for brushing and drizzling

1 quantity Pizza Dough (see page 11), or 1 x 25-cm/ 10-inch pizza base

plain flour, for dusting

6 spinach leaves

1 quantity basic Tomato Sauce (see page 7)

1 tomato, sliced

1 celery stick, thinly sliced

1/2 green pepper, deseeded and thinly sliced

1 baby courgette, sliced

25 g/1 oz asparagus tips

25 g/1 oz sweetcorn, thawed if frozen

4 tbsp peas, thawed if frozen

4 spring onions, trimmed and chopped

1 tbsp chopped fresh mixed herbs

55 g/2 oz mozzarella cheese, grated

2 tbsp freshly grated Parmesan cheese

1 artichoke heart

salt and pepper

vegetable pizza

Preheat the oven to 200°C/400°F/Gas Mark 6. Brush a baking sheet with oil.

Roll out the dough on a lightly floured surface to a 25-cm/ 10-inch round. Place on the baking sheet and push up the edge a little. Cover and let stand in a warm place for 10 minutes.

Remove any tough stalks from the spinach and wash the leaves in cold water. Pat dry with kitchen paper.

Spread the Tomato Sauce over the base of the pizza almost to the edge. Arrange the spinach leaves on top of the sauce, followed by the tomato slices. Top with the remaining vegetables and the fresh mixed herbs.

Combine the cheeses and sprinkle over the pizza. Place the artichoke heart in the centre. Drizzle the pizza with a little olive oil and season to taste.

Bake in the oven for 18–20 minutes or until the edge is crisp and golden brown. Serve immediately.

serves 2–4

55 g/2 oz sun-dried tomatoes
in oil, drained and coarsely
chopped

4 tbsp pine kernels

25 g/1 oz fresh basil leaves

1 garlic clove, chopped

5 tbsp olive oil, plus extra for
brushing

2 tbsp grated Parmesan
cheese

1 quantity Pizza Dough
(see page 11), or 1 x 25-cm/
10-inch pizza base

plain flour, for dusting

85 g/3 oz goat's cheese

85 g/3 oz red cherry
tomatoes, halved

85 g/3 oz yellow cherry
tomatoes, halved

basil, to garnish

salt and pepper

goat's cheese & sun-dried tomato pizza

Put the sun-dried tomatoes, pine kernels, basil and garlic in a food processor or blender and process to a purée. With the motor running, gradually add the olive oil through the feeder tube or hole until thoroughly combined. Scrape into a bowl and stir in the Parmesan. Alternatively, pound the sun-dried tomatoes, pine kernels, basil and garlic to a paste in a mortar with a pestle. Gradually beat in the oil, then stir in the Parmesan. Season lightly with salt and pepper.

Preheat the oven to 200°C/400°F/Gas Mark 6. Brush a baking sheet with oil.

Roll out the dough on a lightly floured surface to a 25-cm/ 10-inch round. Place on the baking sheet and push up the edge a little. Cover and leave to stand in a warm place for 10 minutes.

Spread the sun-dried tomato mixture over the pizza base almost to the edge. Crumble the goat's cheese over it and arrange the tomato halves on top, cut sides up. Bake for 20 minutes, until crisp and golden. Garnish with basil and serve immediately.

serves 2–4

2 tbsp olive oil, plus extra for brushing and drizzling

1 quantity Pizza Dough (see page 11), or 1 x 25-cm/ 10-inch pizza base

plain flour, for dusting

350 g/12 oz spinach

1 onion, thinly sliced

6 tbsp ricotta cheese

1/2 tsp freshly grated nutmeg

2 tbsp pine kernels

115 g/4 oz Fontina cheese, sliced thinly

salt and pepper

ricotta, spinach & pine kernel pizza

Preheat the oven to 220°C/425°F/Gas Mark 7. Brush a baking sheet with oil.

Roll out the dough on a lightly floured surface to a 25-cm/10-inch round. Place on the baking sheet and push up the edge a little. Cover and let stand in a warm place for 10 minutes.

Wash the spinach in cold water and dry well. Heat the oil in a pan, add the onion and cook until soft and translucent. Add the spinach and cook, stirring, until just wilted. Remove the pan from the heat and drain off any liquid.

Spread the ricotta cheese evenly over the pizza base, then cover with the spinach and onion mixture. Sprinkle over the nutmeg and pine kernels and season to taste with salt and pepper. Top with the slices of Fontina and drizzle with olive oil. Bake in the oven for 20–30 minutes, until golden and sizzling. Serve immediately.

serves 2–4

2 tbsp olive oil, plus extra for brushing and drizzling

1 quantity Pizza Dough (see page 11), or 1 x 25-cm/ 10-inch pizza base

plain flour, for dusting

1 quantity basic Tomato Sauce (see page 7)

115 g/4 oz soft cheese

1 tbsp chopped fresh mixed herbs, such as parsley, oregano and basil

225 g/8 oz wild mushrooms, such as oyster, shiitake or ceps, or 115 g/4 oz each wild and button mushrooms

1/4 tsp fennel seeds

4 tbsp roughly chopped walnuts

40 g/11/2 oz blue cheese, of choice

salt and pepper

mushroom & walnut pizza

Preheat the oven to 200°C/400°F/Gas Mark 6. Brush a baking sheet with oil.

Roll out the dough on a lightly floured surface to a 25-cm/ 10-inch round. Place on the baking sheet and push up the edge a little. Cover and let stand in a warm place for 10 minutes.

Carefully spread the Tomato Sauce almost to the edge of the pizza base. Dot with the soft cheese and chopped fresh herbs.

Wipe and slice the mushrooms. Heat the oil in a large frying pan or wok and stir-fry the mushrooms and fennel seeds for 2–3 minutes. Spread over the pizza with the walnuts.

Crumble the blue cheese over the pizza, drizzle with a little olive oil and season with salt and pepper to taste.

Bake in the oven for 18–20 minutes or until the edge is crisp and golden. Serve immediately.

serves 2–4

olive oil, for brushing

1 quantity Pizza Dough
(see page 11), or 1 x 25-cm/
10-inch pizza base

plain flour, for dusting

1 quantity basic Tomato
Sauce (see page 7)

1 aubergine, thinly sliced

175 g/6 oz mozzarella cheese,
sliced

55 g/2 oz black olives,
marinated and stoned

1 tbsp drained capers

4 tbsp freshly grated
Parmesan cheese

2 tbsp olive oil

pizza alla siciliana

Preheat the oven to 200°C/400°F/Gas Mark 6 and brush a baking
sheet with oil.

Roll out the dough on a lightly floured surface to a 25-cm/
10-inch round. Place on the baking sheet and push up the edge
a little. Cover and let stand in a warm place for 10 minutes.

Spread the Tomato Sauce over the pizza base almost to the
edge. Arrange the aubergine slices on top and cover with the
mozzarella. Top with the olives and capers and sprinkle with
the Parmesan. Drizzle with the olive oil.

Bake for 15–20 minutes, or until golden. Serve immediately.

Something
Special

makes 4

2 tbsp olive oil, plus extra for brushing

1 red onion, thinly sliced

1 garlic clove, chopped finely

400 g/14 oz canned tomatoes, chopped

55 g/2 oz black olives, stoned

2 quantities Pizza Dough, combined (see page 11)

plain flour, for dusting

200 g/7 oz mozzarella cheese, drained and diced

1 tbsp chopped fresh oregano

salt and pepper

pizza turnovers

Preheat the oven to 200°C/400°F/Gas Mark 6. Brush a couple of baking sheets with oil.

To make the filling, heat the olive oil in a frying pan. Add the onion and garlic and cook over a low heat, stirring occasionally, for 5 minutes, until softened. Add the tomatoes and cook, stirring occasionally, for a further 5 minutes. Stir in the olives and season to taste with salt and pepper. Remove the frying pan from the heat.

Divide the dough into 4 pieces. Roll out each piece on a lightly floured surface to form a 20-cm/8-inch round.

Divide the tomato mixture among the rounds, spreading it over half of each almost to the edge. Top with the cheese and sprinkle with the oregano. Brush the edge of each round with a little water and fold over the uncovered sides. Press the edges to seal.

Bake for about 15 minutes, until golden and crisp. Remove from the oven and leave to stand for 2 minutes, then transfer to warmed plates and serve.

serves 2–4

2 tbsp olive oil, plus extra for brushing

1 quantity Pizza Dough (see page 11), or 1 x 25-cm/10-inch pizza base

plain flour, for dusting

1 quantity basic Tomato Sauce (see page 7)

70 g/2½ oz cooked shelled prawns

55 g/2 oz artichoke hearts, thinly sliced

25 g/1 oz mozzarella cheese, drained and thinly sliced

1 tomato, thinly sliced

100 g/3½ oz mushrooms or pepperoni, thinly sliced

2 tsp capers, rinsed

2 tsp stoned, sliced black olives

salt and pepper

four seasons pizza

Preheat the oven to 220°C/425°F/Gas Mark 7 and brush a baking sheet with olive oil.

Roll out the dough on a lightly floured surface to a 25-cm/10-inch round. Place on the baking sheet and push up the edge a little. Cover and let stand in a warm place for 10 minutes.

Spread the Tomato Sauce over the pizza base, almost to the edge. Cover one quarter with prawns. Cover a second quarter with artichoke hearts. Cover the third quarter with alternate slices of mozzarella and tomato. Cover the final quarter with the sliced mushrooms or pepperoni. Sprinkle the whole surface with capers and olives, season to taste with salt and pepper, and drizzle with the olive oil.

Bake in the oven for 20–25 minutes, until the crust is crisp and the cheese has melted. Serve immediately.

makes two 23-cm/9-inch pizzas

olive oil, for brushing

1 quantity Pizza Dough (see page 11)

2 courgettes

300 g/10½ oz buffalo mozzarella

1½–2 tbsp finely chopped fresh rosemary, or ½ tbsp dried rosemary

pizza bianca

Preheat the oven to 220°C/425°F/Gas Mark 7. Brush a baking sheet with oil.

Divide the dough in half and shape each half into a ball. Cover 1 ball and roll out the other into a 23-cm/9-inch round. Place the round on a lightly floured baking sheet.

Meanwhile, using a vegetable peeler, cut long, thin strips of courgette. Drain and dice the mozzarella.

Scatter half the mozzarella over the base. Add half of the courgette strips and sprinkle with half of the rosemary. Repeat with the remaining dough and topping ingredients.

Bake the two pizzas in the preheated oven for 15 minutes or until crispy. Serve immediately.

serves 2–4

olive oil, for brushing

1 quantity Pizza Dough
(see page 11), or 1 x 25-cm/
10-inch pizza base

plain flour, for dusting

25 g/1 oz fresh parsley,
chopped

25 g/1 oz fresh basil, chopped

15 g/1/2 oz fresh chives,
chopped

15 g/1/2 oz fresh marjoram,
chopped

2 garlic cloves, finely
chopped

125 ml/4 fl oz sour cream

1 tbsp olive oil flavoured with
mixed herbs

115 g/4 oz Parmesan cheese,
freshly grated

salt and pepper

mixed herbs pizza

Preheat the oven to 200°C/400°F/Gas Mark 6. Brush a baking
sheet with oil.

Roll out the dough on a lightly floured surface to a 25-cm/
10-inch round. Place on the baking sheet and push up the edge a
little. Cover and leave to stand in a warm place for 10 minutes.

Mix together the parsley, basil, chives, marjoram, garlic and sour
cream in a bowl and season with salt and pepper. Brush the pizza
base with the flavoured oil, then spread the herb mixture evenly
over it almost to the edge. Sprinkle with the Parmesan and bake
for 20 minutes, until crisp and golden. Serve immediately.

serves 2–4

6 tbsp olive oil, plus extra for brushing

300 g/10¹/2 oz onions, halved and thinly sliced

50 ml/2 fl oz dry white wine

1 tbsp white wine vinegar

1 tsp lemon juice

70 g/2¹/2 oz rocket, chopped

2 tbsp pine kernels

2 garlic cloves, chopped

30 g/1¹/4 oz Parmesan cheese, freshly grated

1 quantity Pizza Dough (see page 11), or 1 x 25-cm/ 10-inch pizza base

plain flour, for dusting

225 g/8 oz mozzarella cheese, diced

2 tbsp chopped fresh parsley

salt and pepper

caramelized onion & rocket pesto pizza

Heat 2 tablespoons of the oil in a heavy-based saucepan. Add the onions, cover and cook over a very low heat, stirring occasionally, for 1 hour. Increase the heat to medium, uncover the pan and cook until all the liquid has evaporated and the onions are golden brown. Stir in the wine, vinegar and lemon juice, season with salt and pepper and cook, stirring constantly, until the liquid has almost evaporated. Remove the pan from the heat.

Meanwhile, pound the rocket, pine kernels and garlic to a paste with a pestle and mortar. Gradually beat in the oil, then stir in the Parmesan. Alternatively, use a food processor or blender. Season with salt and pepper.

Preheat the oven to 200°C/400°F/Gas Mark 6. Brush a baking sheet with oil. Roll out the dough on a lightly floured surface to a 25-cm/10-inch round. Place on the baking sheet and push up the edge a little. Cover and leave to stand in a warm place for 10 minutes.

Spread the rocket pesto evenly over the pizza base almost to the edge the do the same with the caramelized onions. Sprinkle with the mozzarella and then with the parsley. Drizzle with the remaining olive oil and bake for 20 minutes, until crisp and golden. Serve immediately.

makes 10

1 quantity Pizza Dough
(see page 11)

plain flour, for dusting

1 quantity basic Tomato
Sauce (see page 7)

85 g/3 oz mozzarella cheese,
diced

85 g/3 oz sliced ham, salami
or smoked chicken, cut into
strips

2 fresh marjoram sprigs,
chopped

1 litre/1¾ pints groundnut
oil

deep-fried pizza sandwiches

Divide the dough into 10 pieces and roll out each piece to a round on a lightly floured surface.

Spread the Tomato Sauce evenly over the rounds, leaving a 2-cm/¾-inch margin around the edges. Divide the cheese, meat and marjoram among the rounds. Brush the margins of the rounds with water, fold over the dough and press the edges firmly to seal.

Heat the oil in a deep-fryer or heavy-based saucepan to 180–190°C/350–375°F or until a cube of day-old bread browns in 30 seconds. Add the pizza sandwiches, in batches, and cook for 10 minutes, until crisp and golden brown. Drain well on kitchen paper and keep warm while cooking the remaining batches. Serve hot.

serves 2–4

3 tbsp olive oil

1 onion, chopped

2 garlic cloves, chopped

70 g/2¹/2 oz mushrooms, sliced

1 quantity Pizza Dough (see page 11)

plain flour, for dusting

200 g/7 oz canned sweetcorn, drained

200 g/7 oz canned chopped tomatoes

115 g/4 oz pepperoni sausage, sliced

55 g/2 oz Cheddar cheese, grated

pinch of dried oregano

salt and pepper

upside-down pizza

Preheat the oven to 200°C/400°F/Gas Mark 6.

Heat 2 tbsp of the oil in a 25-cm/10-inch frying pan. Add the onion and cook over a low heat, stirring occasionally, for 5 minutes. Add the garlic and mushrooms and cook, stirring occasionally, for 5 minutes more. Remove the pan from the heat, drain off the oil and leave to cool.

Roll out the dough on a lightly floured surface to a 25-cm/10-inch round. Cover and leave to stand in a warm place for 10 minutes.

Stir the sweetcorn, tomatoes, pepperoni, cheese and oregano into the onion mixture (still in the frying pan) and season with salt and pepper. Place the dough round on top of the filling and tuck in the edge all the way round. Prick a few small holes in the dough to allow steam to escape during cooking and brush with the remaining olive oil. Bake for 18–20 minutes. (If the handle of your frying pan will not withstand the heat of the oven, transfer the mixture to a 25-cm/10-inch round baking tin before adding the dough.)

To serve, place a plate on top of the pizza and, holding the pan and plate firmly together, invert the two. Lift off the pan and serve the pizza immediately.

serves 2–4

olive oil, for brushing

1 quantity Pizza Dough
(see page 11), or 1 x 25-cm/
10-inch pizza base

plain flour for dusting

2 plum tomatoes, diced

2 shallots, diced

175 g/6 oz salmon fillet,
skinned and diced

200 ml/7 fl oz Greek-style
yogurt

4 spring onions, finely
chopped

1 mini cucumber, diced

1 garlic clove, finely chopped

2 tbsp chopped fresh mint

salt and pepper

salmon & tzatziki pizza

Preheat the oven to 200°C/400°F/Gas Mark 6. Brush a baking sheet with oil.

Roll out the dough on a lightly floured surface to a 25-cm/ 10-inch round. Place on the baking sheet and push up the edge a little. Cover and leave to stand in a warm place for 10 minutes.

Sprinkle the tomatoes and shallots evenly over the pizza base almost to the edge. Top with the salmon and season with salt and pepper. Bake for 20 minutes, until crisp and golden.

Meanwhile, make the tzatziki. Lightly whisk the yogurt with a fork in a bowl. Stir in the spring onions, cucumber, garlic and mint and season with salt and pepper.

Remove the pizza from the oven and top with a little of the tzatziki. Serve immediately with the remaining tzatziki.

serves 2–4

olive oil, for brushing

1 fresh red chilli

200 ml/7 fl oz canned coconut milk

1 tbsp red curry paste

1 tbsp soft dark brown sugar

1 tbsp Thai fish sauce

1 lemon grass stalk, lightly crushed

175 g/6 oz skinless boneless chicken breast portion, cut into strips

25 g/1 oz roasted peanuts, ground

1 quantity Pizza Dough (see page 11), or 1 x 25-cm/ 10-inch pizza base

plain flour, for dusting

fresh basil leaves, to garnish

salt and pepper

Thai curry pizza

Preheat the oven to 200°C/400°F/Gas Mark 6. Brush a baking sheet with oil.

Deseed the chilli if you prefer a milder flavour and slice thinly. Heat half the coconut milk in a heavy-based saucepan. Stir in the curry paste and cook, stirring, until it gives off its aroma. Add the sugar, fish sauce and lemon grass and cook, stirring constantly, until the mixture is a rich golden brown colour.

Add the remaining coconut milk and bring back to the boil, then stir in the chicken, peanuts and chilli. Lower the heat and simmer for 10–15 minutes, until most of the liquid has evaporated.

Roll out the dough on a lightly floured surface to a 25-cm/ 10-inch round. Place on the baking sheet and push up the edge a little. Cover and leave to stand in a warm place for 10 minutes.

Remove the pan from the heat. Remove and discard the lemon grass and season the curry to taste with salt and pepper. Spoon the curry on to the pizza base, spreading it out almost to the edge. Bake for 20 minutes, until crisp and golden, and serve immediately, garnished with basil leaves.

serves 2–4

butter, for greasing

1 quantity Pizza Dough
(see page 11) combined with
55 g/2 oz cocoa powder

plain flour, for dusting

125 ml/4 fl oz milk

175 g/6 oz curd cheese

85 g/3 oz caster sugar

1 small egg, lightly beaten

1 tsp ground ginger

4 tbsp flaked almonds

200 g/7 oz canned or bottled
Morello cherries, drained

chocolate cherry pizza

Preheat the oven to 190°C/375°F/Gas Mark 5. Grease a 25-cm/
10-inch shallow cake tin with butter.

Turn out the dough on to a lightly floured surface and knead
lightly. Roll out lightly to a 27–cm/10¾-inch round and lift into
the tin, pressing it against the sides and evenly over the base.

To make the topping, mix together the cheese, sugar and egg in
a bowl, beating well with a fork. Stir in the ground ginger and
set aside.

Sprinkle half the almonds over the pizza base, add the cheese
mixture and bake for 15 minutes. Put the cherries on top of the
cheese mixture, sprinkle with the remaining almonds and return
to the oven for a further 10–15 minutes. Serve hot or cold.